Y0-BVQ-840

CAPRICORN HOROSOPE 2015

Lisa Lazuli

©Lisa Lazuli – all rights reserved

No part of this book may be reproduced without author's permission

Published in London 2014

Lisa Lazuli is the author of the amazon bestseller

HOROSCOPE 2014: ASTROLOGY and NUMEROLOGY HOROSCOPES

ABOUT THE AUTHOR

Lisa Lazuli studied astrology with the Faculty of Astrological Studies in London.

She has practiced since 1999.

Lisa has been a regular guest on BBWM and BBC Shropshire talking about astrology and doing both horoscopes and live readings. She has also made guest appearances on Fox FM, BBC Cambridgeshire, BBC Northamptonshire, BBC Coventry and Warwickshire and US Internet Radio Shows including the Debra Clement Show.

Lisa wrote horoscopes for Asian Woman Magazine.

Now available in eBook and paperback:

TAURUS: Your Day, Your Decan, Your Sign *The most REVEALING book on The Bull yet.* Includes 2015 Predictions.

ARIES HOROSCOPE 2015

TAURUS HOROSCOPE 2015

GEMINI HOROSCOPE 2015

CANCER HOROSCOPE 2015

LEO HOROSCOPE 2015

VIRGO HOROSCOPE 2015

LIBRA HOROSCOPE 2015

SCORPIO HOROSCOPE 2015

SAGITTARIUS HOROSCOPE

Lisa Lazuli is also the author of

The mystery/thrillers:

A Sealed Fate

Holly Leaves

Next of Sin

As well as:

Delicious, Nutritious Recipes for the Time and Cash Strapped

Paleo Diet: Get Started, Get Motivated, Feel Great.

99 ACE Places to Promote Your Book

Pressure Cooking Reinvented.

FOREWARD

Dear Reader,

I hope my yearly horoscopes will provide you with some insightful guidance during what is a very tricky time astrologically speaking with the heavy planets i.e. Pluto and Uranus at loggerheads in cardinal signs and Neptune in Pisces calling us all to get in touch with our spiritual side.

I have a conversational style of writing, please excuse any grammatical errors, I write much as I would speak.

As the song goes, "Nobody said it was easy." I know the mass media pump-out shows us plenty about quick fix love, money, fame and success; however, life is a journey filled with challenges and obstacles designed to encourage us to find out what we are made of and who we really are.

Embrace the good and bad and enjoy what is your unique experience.

Be the hero in your own personal life movie and never hide your spotlight.

I must add that the best astrology insights are gained from a unique chart based on your time, date, year and place of birth.

If you would like your natal chart calculated for FREE, click here:

http://lisalazuli.com/2014/06/30/would-you-like-to-know-where-all-your-planets-are-free-natal-chart/

Please join me on Facebook:

https://www.facebook.com/pages/Lisa-Lazuli-Astrologer/192000594298158?ref=hl

Contents

Overview

2015 is a year of significant, inspiring and often surprising changes. It is a time of beginning adventures and revolutionizing your life. 2015 is right in the middle of a period when Capricorns have been challenged to shake up the status quo, to close chapters and to open new ones. As a cardinal sign, you are naturally forward looking and while you like, as an earth sign, to have everything organized and arranged, you are always itching for new horizons and for new mountains to climb. Capricorn, unlike the other earth signs – Taurus and Virgo, who can be passive – is a sign that strives, that never settles, and which always seeks more, and that is why the changes symbolized by Pluto in your sign are not a threat, but something you welcome.

Pluto can give to you an awesome power to achieve and to restructure your life. They say, "If it ain't broke don't fix it," but that saying does not allow for improvement and fine tuning, and it encourages averageness, and if there is anything Capricorns do not like it is being average. 2015 is a time when you are not scared to tear things up and start again, rebuilding your life, your career, your home, your car, etc. to make something which works better, performs better and creates more value for you.

Capricorn are one of the signs who are most honest about life and about themselves, but this year what you learn about yourself can be surprising even to you – the superficial is being stripped away and any veneers you have used to cover up truths about how you feel and who you are will be shattered. By getting more in touch with who you are, you can make better decisions and see clearly which goals are most worth pursuing and what really needs addressing in your life. This year is a part of a period in which your whole life direction is changing, and even your personality is undergoing a shift. Not everyone will have a Pluto conjunct or even opposite or square their Sun in a lifetime, and so the opportunity it gives for constructive change is one not to be missed. The conjunction is far more beneficial than the square and opposition as you have more control over the changes and are able to catch the wave and go with it, rather than being an unwilling piece of driftwood being tossed about by the waves.

This is very much a time to take control of your life, and taking control should not mean being controlling and trying to micromanage every aspect of your life and relationships in order to avoid any changes. The comfort zone is the biggest threat to our potential: as soon as we reach a certain level of achievement or a certain position in life, we start protecting what we have. We almost pull up the drawbridge and become resistant to anything that threatens what we now have. Once, or maybe twice in a lifetime, the planets come and break all that up; they destroy our comfort zones and create events to invade our fortresses of complacency. Yes, we can see these events as shocking and disruptive, but they can free up our potentials again, creating opportunity for us to rediscover ourselves and find a happier and more fulfilled way of living we never thought of. Capricorn can feel this zest for change stirring within them, and you are ready to go with it and to embrace it. Although you dislike risk and the unknown, you are more willing now to take risks and plunge into the unknown.

Repressing feelings and living in the past is not an option now; soon a chapter will slam shut and you will not be able to mull over the pages of the past chapter wishing you could re-write it. Consign guilt and disappointment to that past chapter and get writing the script for the next best years of your life.

If you are in denial about your true feelings for situations or people, your subconscious can trigger events that can subversively challenge your conscious motives. Have you ever been really angry with someone but kept that anger in and pretended it was fine, then suddenly something unconnected happened, and that person exploded at you and the argument you tried to avoid happened anyway? Often our subconscious 'arranges' events that our conscious is trying to avoid – our subconscious is more in tune with what we really want and need while our conscious mind is often conditioned to act or behave in a certain way. Recognize your urges and react positively in addressing them rather than being complicit with fate in allowing others or events to precipitate what you shied away from.

It is time to step out of someone else's shadow

Pluto brings you the power to create and destroy – you may destroy those structures in your life that block the possibilities for growth and enjoyment in life.

Career and identity are very important to you this year, and you may seek to change your career or to use your professional abilities to pursue a life path that is more reflective of who you want to be seen as. It is also important for you to feel that you are out there in the world – self-employment, being a housewife, being a student or being retired may no longer appeal to you, and you may seek a role that gives you a greater feeling of identity and more visibility. If you work in the background or behind the scenes, this may be the year you discover that you have leadership talent that is underused within your current role. Capricorn make very good leaders, even though you do not seek leadership as actively as other signs.

This year is one where your organization skills, especially to do with financial affairs, are well honed, and you can focus effort and manage resources. If you are starting a new business, this is an excellent time as you are able to do all the number crunching in order to produce the detailed forecasts, budgets and cash flow projections that you may need to get loans or rent property. Your head is about you with figures. This is also an outstanding year for those who use their memory a lot, i.e. learning lines if you act, if you give speeches and presentations often, or if you need to present sales fugues to your boss and have to be able to rattle off numbers from memory. If you do decide to take on a job with the roles mentioned above, you can do very well.

This is a great year to increase your financial understanding or take a job where you have more control over and responsibility for money. You may take on a course in accounting, bookkeeping, financial management or investment so that you can apply for a different role within your company or a new job altogether.

You are a careful thinker but can make bold and courageous decisions. 2015 is a very effective year for managing people and getting the most from them within teams or your business. You will find that your ability to make friends, build bridges and get on with even difficult people is enhanced. You have the ability to make deals, gain cooperation and negotiate very powerfully.

You may face some changes and disruptions to your life via the company you work with or your boss – restructuring within your company or the sudden retirement of your boss, may come out of the blue and may cause you to change job or change your job description. You may have to travel away from home, or even live away from home for part of the year due to your job. This can be a very exciting change, which may well enable you to discover that you actually like living in the new place and want to make it permanent.

Friendship is very important to you this year, and you will make many new and long-lasting friends. If you are single, then romance is very likely to be found with a friend or someone a friend introduces you to. This is a very good year for love in that the bonds you form with a new partner will be strong and durable, and the relationship will be down to earth and pleasant, with an immediate sense of being comfortable with each other. Marriages and existing relationships will benefit from your easy going, compromising attitude and your willingness to communicate about issues of the heart. Capricorn can be rather stoic in love: reliable, dependable and responsible, but you guys are not always eager to chat about matters of the heart, and often you balk at romantic gestures. This year you are in touch with your romantic side and eager to chat about how and where the relationship is going and what you can do to make things better. Events this year are quite chaotic, but they can bring you and your loved one together as you are on this journey of adventure together. Family life can be directed and influenced by your career this year, but it is possible to create a balance where everyone is a winner. Friendship and communication are very important to you now, and sexually and emotionally you want to open up and talk about sex, intimacy, love, fantasies, role play, experimentation, etc. You are interested in adding a new dimension to your love life: sexually you are driven to please your partner, and your partner will respond with interest. Being more open and more spontaneous in life will mean your love life is red hot in 2015.

2015 is an excellent year to take your health and fitness into hand as for one, you are more motivated than usual; two, you have more energy than usual, and three, you are very pro-active and positive. Use the extra energy surge you are getting courtesy of the planets to devote more time to sport and to read up about diets that may suit you and your lifestyle. If you want to make a radical change like going vegan or quitting alcohol or trying any other healthy lifestyle – go for it, it can be life-changing.

For those of you regularly involved in sports, you are very competitive this year and can win and achieve personal bests. You may be selected to tour with your team overseas. Teamwork can be very inspiring for you this year, whether it is for sport or for another project, and you can get rather geed up – do remember to be inclusive of everyone's ideas and of the vested interests at stake in the group. Your vigor and can-do attitude this year are great, but can lead you to step on toes at times inadvertently.

Capricorn are known to be rather conservative and cautious; however, this year a far more adventurous you is coming to the fore. You are more likely to embrace new concepts and idea and to follow paths which may lead nowhere, but which you somehow need to explore. This openness extends to new relationships with lovers and friends, where you will open up quickly to people you don't usually relate to.

While this is a very productive year with some big things to tackle and get used to, it is also a year filled with fun. A strong sense of purpose and also a sense of humor is allowing you to see the lighter side of every experience.

There is a very big focus on you this year: you take center stage, and you have the power to change those things about life that no longer work. 2015 is about new beginnings and creating organization out of chaos as only a Capricorn can. It is time to break old habits and molds and create a new template for success with solid plans and positive actions. New starts often come out of surprise events, and your ability to use foresight, willfulness and creativity can help you to adapt and quickly excel in the new environment. This is a year where you will feel motivated and enthusiastic about your life – life is exciting again and filled with possibility. 2015 is one of fire in your belly and love in your heart: your sense of humor and tenderness towards others will ensure you make good friends and that your love life fulfills, stimulates and nourishes you.

LIFE

You enter 2015 in a good mood and high spirits; you are tired of holidays and are eager to get going and to get busy. You will hit the ground running and make immediate headway with projects and chores.

You have a way of communicating this month that is fluent, easy going and that wins cooperation and trust. You are quite charming and can use this charm to make an impression in business or with people you meet for the first time.

Relationships with siblings can be both pleasant and supportive emotionally right now – blood is thicker than water, and these relationships will strengthen. Pleasant trips and get-togethers are common this month, and you will use your creative flair in entertaining your guests.

Your desire is strong this month – when you want something, you want it now! Impatience is counter-productive, and you need to be measured as some things cannot be rushed – think more about timing. Even if you are thorough, is now the best time to be doing these things you are so anxious to do? Ask yourself: what is the rush, and why is there a rush? If there is no answer, take that as a cue to hold back and wait for more information or feedback before proceeding.

No matter how persuasive you are, some people will not be cajoled, and you must know when to back off.

Healthwise you may take things to extremes this month: at one end of the scale you may be pigging out or at the other end you may overdo the exercise, bran and smoothies – moderation and common sense is the key.

LOVE

You are sensitive and responsive to the needs of those around you; you are eager to please and reluctant to hurt feelings, which may mean you brush things under the carpet. However, a word of warning, do not brush aside now incidents and angers that are likely to resurface, as when they do resurface they may do so explosively. Nip any problems in the bud now and set boundaries, even though you are in a giving mood. A very good month for constructive talk in relationships and for turning over a new leaf – i.e. recommitting to the relationship by agreeing to put in extra effort and to be more accommodating. Relationships need work, and this month extra effort you put in will get results and be very rewarding. Sometimes rules and boundaries in relationships help create security and respect, and this month you will have to recognise that.

A very good month for Capricorns looking to meet new partners – people really feel as if they can open up to you and thus a rapport and a genuine closeness can develop quickly. Capricorns are looking to meet partners who have potential this year as you are seeking stability emotionally and will be less likely to pursue relationships that are shakey and problematic. People you attract now may be mature (not necessarily older but wiser) and financially organised with a settled life.

CAREER

An ability to be persuasive and tactful can assist you in swinging any situation your way. This is a very profitable time in business when lucrative deals and new contacts can be made; the one danger is that you may not know when to back off. In business and love as well, coming on too strong is a major turn off and so do not fall into that trap.

Remember that everyone can work together if everyone wins – you need to make sure that everyone is on board by selling your plans to everyone involved, do not come across as self-interested.

This is a very good month to take on new workers in your business or hire temporary staff – your workload is expanding, and it is an opportune time to hire good people.

An urge to take a stand and stick up for what you believe in, could put you at odds with other leader figures at work or within the wider community, but you have the courage of your convictions right now, and even if the nail that sticks out is the first to be hit, you'll still want to be that nail. You may be the 1st business owner or professional in your field to take a view that is different or liberal and act on it. You want to put your money where you mouth is, and so if that means resisting pressure to cut wages, holiday pay, sell unethically produced products or products that harm the planet, that is what you will do. Making money is important to you, but principles and value are more important, even if that makes you out of step with your industry.

LIFE

This month saving and making cutbacks is essential – do not leave yourself short at the end of the month. Budgeting and money management are essential – you may have to borrow from Peter to give to Paul so to speak. Capricorns are renowned for their ability to save and balance their finances, but unexpected expenses from the end of the last month/start of Feb may throw your monthly money map out of sync. You are, however, very skilful and original in the ways you arrange money or earn extra money. This month is especially good for creating money-making opportunities via the internet i.e. Amazon Associates, Google AdSense, affiliate programs, eBay, etc. You may do a good clear-out of the loft or basement and find things you do not want, which you can sell to raise money.

This is a good month for picking something up cheap at a sale or bric-a-brac shop and selling it on for a good profit – somehow you are able to see value in something which another has discarded and you can use that ability to turn a profit.

Capricorns are very artistic, and not many of you know that as The Goat is not associated with art – this is a very good month to discover that talent or to make more use of it. Your talents can be directed towards dress making, cordon bleu cooking or interior design – you may even begin a new business idea to do with these activities.

You have a great deal of confidence in social situations this month – you can be charming and effervescent quite naturally, so this month is perfect for business mingling and networking, staff bonding and making friends fast in new situations.

LOVE

Like people, relationships are unique, and one should accept and enjoy the quirks and randomness of your relationship without trying to force yourself into a mold of what you perceive as 'normal' or 'unusual'. This year your close love relationship or marriage will be more dynamic, and your routines and lifestyle may change for you as a couple. This may mean one of you working nights or one of you working away more. A new baby etc. will create a total change in your relationship from a practical point of view, and this month you will have to figure it all out, it may be just what you both need in an inverse way. The new routines may create more freedom and actually bring you closer.

This is a very good month for couples who work together in business, and even if you do not currently work together, you may start to think about it, since many Capricorns are beginning businesses this year, it makes sense that you should do so with your loved one.

This may be a month of discovery in even long-term relationships where you learn something you never knew about your partner – it can be something intriguing, and you will wonder why you had never noticed or asked about it before.

Single and attached Capricorns will have a very fun-filled Valentine's Day – this year it's more about laughs and fun than cozy romance and quiet nights at the fire. You may socialize with friends on Valentine's Day. A very good month for romance as you are communicating very well and are confident in yourself.

CAREER

If your run your own business or are in partnership, this month you must pay more attention to how you come across – what does your reception area look like, how quickly do you answer calls, how fast do you return calls, do you update clients, are all your staff friendly and polite, does your coffee machine work – these factors can cost your business if you do not make sure they are smart and efficient. Appearances and first impressions can be make or break in February.

and so in whichever field you work in, make sure your hair, hygiene and clothes look sharp – do not yawn, and pay attention to body language. We should not judge books by their covers, but this month people will judge you in this way, and so take note and remember what Karl Lagerfeld said, "A respectable appearance is sufficient to make people more interested in your soul."

If you work in confectionary, a coffee shop, children's entertainment, stationery, greetings cards or a salon this can be an excellent month for business. If you are looking to start a business or looking for a job, these are some ideas for you.

This is also a very positive month for those who work from home or who are starting businesses to run from home – your motivation and energy are very high, and you can achieve a great volume of work. If you are currently employed, but have a skill, you may decide to quit the job and do what you do from home instead.

LIFE

Learning is important this month, but what you do not want to do is think you know something and then go on the hunt for people who agree with you or look for facts which support what you already think. True learning is about challenging our ideas, and this month you should not cling to any opinions or theories which are outdated. Information is coming at you quickly, and you need to be adaptable in your thinking – old methods of dealing with things may not work, and you need to widen your options.

If you have been putting something off, now is the time to tackle it – it may be an essay or letter you need to write, a form you need to fill out, or errand you need to run. You may actually be putting something off for no good reason at all – the best way is to tackle it and get it sorted out before the thing you are putting off becomes an even bigger hurdle in your mind. If this thing you are putting off involves telling someone something difficult, be very tactful, the longer you leave it the harder it will be, and so act now because delaying may well be harming the other person, as well.

It is a nervy month where you can feel anxious and then suddenly excited for no reason, being quite jumpy you may overreact to certain small occurrences and say something you later regret. A decision made in haste is a bad one, and there is a big difference between doing something timeously and rushing it.

This month will be filled with variety, and you will meet many new people. Communication is a theme in both business and your personal life – but focus on quality, not quantity.

LOVE

This month you really need to make an effort to listen and that does not mean saying, “Yeah honey, I’m listening!” while you are simultaneously scolding the dog, making dinner and looking at your phone. Quality communication means giving someone your undivided attention, and while you cannot always understand or agree with someone, you can at least take time to take their concerns and thoughts on board.

Love and relationships can be difficult this month, not due to major disagreements, but due to stress, workload and logistical issues that leave you with no time for each other. It is also hard to get what you want from your partner when you do not know what you want either – you can be very erratic emotionally this month, and that is sending out mixed signals to your loved one leading to general confusion. You also have a tendency to make too much of something that is very insignificant, and you can also be rather dismissive of anything you see as unimportant.

The best way to enjoy this month is to get out socially with your partner and go somewhere totally new to you both – somewhere stimulating and exciting where you can get away from everything mundane and stressful. In day-to-day life, try not to be snappy and explain when you are tired and stressed and need time to yourself. Most people understand better when you explain why you are acting in a certain way, so communicate about your stresses and worries – a problem shared is a problem halved this month.

Be aware of a certain passive aggression this month which is driving events in your relationship without you really being conscious of it.

CAREER

The tempo at work is fast this month, and you will have to deal with more information, people and paperwork than usual. If you are studying now, the intensity of learning will go up a notch, and you will need to focus on your studies. Avoid distractions this month and keep your eye on the ball – it is one of those months where with so much happening and you being pulled in many different directions with competing responsibilities, things can get overlooked.

Keep notes and check your diary to avoid feeling out of control. A sibling or retired close relative may be able to help you with some tasks at work or home to help you cope.

Travel nationally is very possible with your work, and it may be arranged last minute. You can achieve much this month, but even though it is hectic, the pace is not an excuse to drop the quality of your output or to be careless, especially when it comes to what you write, to logistics or research of facts. You must be very clear of facts and figures in your work – make sure any facts you rely on are accurate and up-to-date.

You may have to coordinate a large number of people in March: make sure you have every email and phone number for these people so that you can contact them about last minute changes, send out memos and make sure that no one can say, "I never knew" or "No one told me that!"

In speeches, presentations and essays – be succinct and to the point. You do not have to go on forever, saying something pertinent and powerful can be more effective than a long drawn out piece.

LIFE

You may feel the need to put on a brave front this month as you are feeling vulnerable and quite touchy inside. This is not a month when you will be able to take criticism on board easily, and you should shy away from situations or people where you are likely to be put down. What you don't need this month is negativity – stay away from the Debbie Downers, who seek to cast a shadow over everything. Sometimes you just need positivity around you, and you need to hear some compliments, and so make sure you surround yourself with upbeat people who are encouraging and who focus on the glass half full. Constructive criticism can also be a bad thing if there is too much of it without a balancing dose of encouragement.

In April, recreation and entertainment are very important – they say work is the rent we pay for life, and yet very often we end up paying that rent and never living. This month it is essential for you to get to work on having fun and letting your hair down. If something is not going your way, just drop it and forget all about it – this is not a month when plugging away gets you anywhere, mental breathers and a change of environment are what you need.

Sports and also mental games i.e. crosswords/Sudoku are an ideal outlet for you. If you have creative hobbies or work in an industry where you are artistic, you should have a large amount of energy to put behind new projects. Fresh air and the outdoors is very important right now – you need sunshine and to be active for your overall health.

Children's parties, organizing children within something like a sports team, scouts/guides or teaching children sports and life skills can be a big part of the month. You may be instrumental in helping a child you know gain confidence or hone a skill.

LOVE

Children are very important this month, and you and your partner may become closer in the way you both educate and support your children. But it is not only the children who are important, it is rediscovering the child within yourself and learning to accept and love that inner child. This month it is very important to re-examine the negative messages you may have received from adults about yourself as a child and how they affect you today. Sometimes even a careless or un-factual comment about ourselves we heard as a child can stick in our heads and plague us later in life. Perhaps something your own child is experiencing now or a phase they are going through will allow you to relive your own experience and thereby put a positive spin on it and consign any neuroses that stemmed from it to the past. Maybe helping your own child (or a child in your family) overcome something you suffered with can help you get resolution. These events to do with children can have a very positive effect on your own self-esteem, and that will help relationships.

There is an issue this month with identity and self-love – the stronger your identity, and the better you treat yourself, the better love life and sex life will be. If you are too hard on yourself that may be feeding poor self-esteem, which is damaging your relationships. Focusing on pleasurable activities that reaffirm who you are and what you love about life, is the perfect way to put yourself into a positive frame of mind which will certainly aid both new and old relationships. Do not be afraid to have fun and have lots of it!

It is vital that your partner is supportive and loving this month – if he/she is negative, you need to make a stand and chastise them for being judgmental and not understanding.

CAREER

Cultivating good relations with co-workers is vital to smooth running of affairs – be tactful, be helpful, and go the extra mile to get along with others.

Bargaining and negotiating are a big part of this month's work effort, and you will have to be creative in coming up with new plans and new ideas until you can reach agreement – prepare for meeting with plans A, B, C and D.

You may be called upon to deal with difficult customers or clients and use your skills with people to take a strong yet fair approach and get this resolved. Your analytical skills are excellent this month, and this can enable you to find solutions to problems by examining figures, trends, anomalies and research. You can also use your intuitive business powers to suss out new opportunities.

Your work may bring you into contact with children via social work, legal work or human rights work – you can make some very valuable progress here by taking a strong leadership role to ensure something does get done rather than talk talk with no walk walk.

LIFE

This is a time where you can be very confused, and it is impossible to follow your intuition as it is sending you mixed messages. You are best not making major decisions or instigating any important discussions as you are just not in tune right now – you feel off kilter as if you are a radio station with a scratchy signal. Back to basics is the advice – stick to the tried and tested for the moment and concentrate on the essential. Keep things and plans simple as the more elaborate things are, the more likely they are to go wrong.

In health, look after your chest as ear, nose, throat and chest infections can strike now – eat loads of onions, garlic, leeks and oranges, and if you feel a cold coming on, get rest immediately.

You may have less energy this month and so do not plan anything that is highly taxing or physically strenuous, conserve energy where you can and just say NO to extra hours or late nights at the office. This is a time when no matter how much effort you put in, results in the short run cannot be guaranteed, and so know when to quit and leave it for another day.

Life is not linear, it is more like snakes and ladders, and sometimes if you push too hard in a direction resistance builds up – this month take your foot off the gas and take the pressure off yourself. Make time to relax and participate in an activity that gives back to you i.e. horse riding, dog walking, playing the piano, practicing your golf swing, etc.

LOVE

One-to-one relationships are important to you this month, and you will prefer to spend time alone with your partner or spouse rather than socializing with friends – you are not in the mood for hubbub or bickering, you just want a peaceful, harmonious atmosphere. You may just agree or go along with things being as flexible as you can to ensure you get the sense of tranquility you require. If your partner is hell-bent on arguing, you are best avoiding him/her and going off quietly by yourself to think. Nothing can be achieved by arguing or even debating right now as you may complicate things unnecessarily.

This has the potential to be a wonderful time in love partnerships if you can just switch off from the mundane hassles and escape to a bubble of calm where romance and love can thrive. This is definitely a month where you and your partner need to say, "OK what is important here and what isn't; let's cut the crap out of our lives, blow some people off, take off the phone and have each other all to ourselves!" We often get bogged down in obligations and engagements that offer us nothing – focus on what you both really enjoy doing, and please each other, not anyone else.

Capricorns in new relationships may find that their feelings are changing rapidly about the other person, and that they are giving out mixed messages – you are quite entitled to have mixed feelings as long as you do not allow things to become too intense, focus on the friendship and fun side of your new relationship; if it is already getting very dark with feelings of control or jealousy setting in from the other person, cool it off.

CAREER

Expect your routine to be thrown out by unforeseeable snags and hitches. These problems may actually be indicative of something bigger going on and so do not ignore them, investigate them and use them as an opportunity to iron out a bigger potential problem down the line.

This is not an ideal month to put big plans into action as ongoing projects will provide you with enough work. If, however, you have just started something new, there will be teething problems no matter how well you have prepared, and this should not frustrate you. It should rather motivate you to achieve more perfection and fine tuning.

In financial matters and also if you work in fields like building, architecture, components, surveying, building products of high specification etc., do not cut corners and do be patient, things cannot be rushed right now.

Colleagues can be rather unreliable and even irritating this month – issues in their own personal lives may leave them performing under par, and you may have to pick up the pieces.

It can be easy to forget the longer term goals and plans due to the disruptions of this year, but keep your eye on the prize and stay calm.

LIFE

This is a far better month for decisive action and making strides towards goals. You can be very organized and highly effective and efficient racing through chores and jobs.

You are quite serious this month and wish to cut through any nonsense and get right into the nitty gritty. This is a very good month for technical writing or for giving speeches or presentations which are meant to be instructive and informative – you have an ability to package your message in a way that is easy for the listener to digest and understand. In journalism or academic writing, you are very good at editing and reducing the information down to make it fit the columns or word counts.

You are very realistic this month and are very good at pacing yourself and preparing diligently – your solid approach to what you do will ensure progress.

You are very good at making sense of subtle and almost unperceivable emotions and tensions in the environment, especially within relationships (marriage and personal); your ability to understand what is being said between the lines can give you an advantage in both dealing with difficult people or coming to solutions to interpersonal problems. You can use your highly attuned sixth sense to suss out situations and people and act more appropriately or timeously than others, giving you an advantage. Your ability to tap into the undercurrents in social thought can enable you to write very powerful literature or speeches.

Relationships in general are very intense this month and can be the means by which you evolve psychologically.

LOVE

You can have a great effect on your partner with your words – you will know the right words to say to comfort, to romance or to show your compassion. Your ability to both understand deeper emotions and broach them in a rational way can help relationships resolve issues and run more smoothly. Sexual problems can also be discussed in a dispassionate and helpful way. Everyone wants to be understood, and your ability to listen and understand even without someone explaining to you in words of one syllable will enhance love and the bond you have together.

Driving factors that you have not been aware of, but which are dictating the course of the relationship can come to light now and be recognized and dealt with.

The sexual side of both new and old relationships is important as there is an increased intensity and desire. Sexual healing is possible where if the sex is going well it can actually bring you together and help you move beyond other issues. Sex is more than just sex this month – it is an avenue for self-transformation and self-expression as it can relax you and help you to open up.

CAREER

This is a very good month for administrators and those who are running businesses – you can be very effective at streamlining or re-organizing to make things more economical. This is also a great month for proofreaders, editors, financial controllers, teachers and auditors. You can excel at anything requiring skill and precision, but you are best working alone as you are not likely to be patient with others. You need to be able to work at your own tempo; if you have to work in a team where progress relies on the commitment of others, you can become highly frustrated.

You have good concentration and focus, and that means that you can direct your energy towards detail work. You can achieve good results right now, and hard work will result in concrete dividends.

You are highly creative and can have many fruitful ideas, which you can turn into useful or money-making projects.

In your own business, you may have to let someone go if they are not providing value for money.

This can be an excellent month to apply for a loan. You may get a tax refund or tax break as well, or there may be a tax break as a result of a loan or investment you make.

LIFE

Your energy levels are back in credit this month, and you are feeling like you are in the starting blocks, raring to go. One problem can be directing your energies in a way that is productive, rather than doing a bit of this and a bit of that or starting so many things that you follow through on none of them. You must outline your plans carefully and draw up a plan of action rather than just jumping into things and going with the flow. Expansion within structure is the theme – the structures should not limit or inhibit you, but rather help you to be focused and systematic.

The need to prove yourself is very strong, and this can lead you to promise more than you can deliver or bite off more than you can chew – which is why you need to have a clear plan and must not underestimate any task at hand. There is no doubt that you can achieve a lot, but it should be done incrementally as you go, not going in headlong and then losing the plot as things get too chaotic.

This is a month when you will have to be competitive – you will come head to head with others to compete for a job, a promotion, a prize or an award, and competition will be fierce. You are assertive and will not give in; your positive frame of mind should win you the day.

LOVE

Your needs and what satisfies you may be changing this month, and that may lead to you drifting apart from your partner this month, not in a negative way, but it may be you need more space to explore who you are. If we are allowed space in a relationship to be a free spirit occasionally, we can take so much more back to that relationship when we 'return'. You need your partner to indulge you this month, and whether you need to read more, see more of your friends, go hiking, cycling, bird watching etc., you should be able to follow your desire. It may even be that your religion calls you, and you feel the need to get closer to the church – whatever it is, you have a calling this month which could temporarily cause you to drift apart; however it will, if you are allowed that freedom, enrich the relationship long-term.

Single Capricorn could meet lovers with excellent potential via university, an awareness campaign, a seminar to do with health or animal rights movements.

CAREER

Working in groups can be rather challenging as you are very adamant about how things should be done and can find it hard to work to timescales and rules set by others. You work best where you have freedom to direct your part of the job as you see fit – if you do not have that freedom, you may just rush the job to get finished as fast as possible.

This is a very good month for projects to do with politics, social matters or the community, where you are able to feel as if the impact of your work has a wider effect on lives and futures. Many Capricorns work in law, law enforcement or in government, and this month you may be able to create far reaching changes via the work you are putting in. Whatever you do for a living, there is the feeling of wanting to give more back and for it not to be just about the pay check. Teaching new colleagues or trainees at the office can give you some satisfaction, you may take a younger colleague under your wing and help them to develop.

LIFE

All good literature is driven by confrontation and in life too, inner transformation, i.e. the story of our lives is driven by confrontation that is not always blatant. Analyze the subtle and the more obvious incidents in your life this month where you confront people or even fears. Often we draw to us people who reflect in us what we need to acknowledge and accept. The more we repress and deny aspects of ourselves or our personality, the more they control us by unconsciously directing our actions. Look closely at the people you attract right now, and who you lock horns with – what can they teach you about yourself?

This is also a month of turnarounds – someone you once trusted and cared about may disappoint you, and you may part ways, alternatively, you may develop a close bond with a person you had previously hated. What lies beneath is very important right now – the hidden motivations and desires. What makes you hate someone may also be what could ultimately attract you to them.

You may have an odd feeling that something is missing: something that you used to enjoy has been lost. Perhaps keeping up with commitments and routines has led you to neglect doing something you really cared about, something that made you feel fulfilled – you must get back to that activity as perhaps some of the confrontation is driven by an inner frustration that you are losing part of yourself in the hubbub of modern life.

Health insurance for travel is vital – make sure you have it. A health or dental issue may arise on holiday and so make sure you are covered – nothing serious, just be prepared.

LOVE

Strong emotions and intensity of feeling can make relationships both passionate and rocky this month. You are not in a compromising mood, and you will not let things lie, which can lead to heated debates especially when it comes to money issues and matters of principle. However, much of your passion is driven by strength of feeling and commitment to making the relationship work. You are very protective and will react strongly to any perceived threat to your happiness or your family. You may subconsciously try and stir things up in the relationship as a way of gaging the depth of feeling of your partner.

Jealousy from both sides is an issue this month, so is control and subtle mind games – once in a while we all play these, but it is not Capricorn's style, and it makes you uncomfortable. This is, however, a passing phase and is merely a result of the strong emotions that have arisen, and which are not easy to understand. Changes in your life in general are impacting on the more intimate parts of your life, and a desire to protect this part from the changes can bring out this controlling urge.

Even new relationships can be profound in the effect they have on you: Capricorns are private people, but you will want to open up quickly to your new love interest, and you can develop a deeper bond because of this.

Sex can be excellent this month, even though it is driven by a strange cocktail of love, lust and obsession.

CAREER

Managing money and resources is part of this month. You may be given responsibility for managing funds, anything from a hedge fund or petty cash. It is not so much about managing your own money, but being given the responsibility to look after, invest or hold in trust a sum of money. You must keep accurate records and be as transparent as possible.

Knowing how to deal with tricky situations is also very important, and the line between right and wrong could get very blurred. You may have to keep a secret to protect your client or a colleague, and while this may not sit easily with you, it may be the only option.

In your business, you must organize the day-to-day running of your company to accommodate the changes and plans you have for the future – if you want to expand/sell overseas, now is the time to talk to your bank about foreign currency accounts, forward rates or anything else, i.e. insurance for goods in transit, trade laws or other bureaucratic issues that could affect you.

You may have to deal with colleagues or staff members who are not as keen as you are on the changes that you are proposing or that are required, and you may have to help motivate or even train them in order to convince them it's a good idea. New training or further education to do with changes in your workplace i.e. streamlining, restructuring etc., could result in you attending a night school or college course.

LIFE

This is a key month for the changes, and themes talked about in the overview. Unexpected events will test your commitment to the path you have chosen as well as giving you a chance to make changes you need the push to make.

We all have different views about fate and destiny – I believe in choice rather than chance, we are, in the main, masters of our destiny, and yet sometimes fate does step in to give us the nudge we may need, and you need to see events this month in that context.

House moves, home renovations or living away from home is possible this month. This is also a time many Capricorns may fly the nest, leaving home or renting or buying their own first home. Along this theme, Capricorns may leave their hometown or home country in order to seek new opportunities to earn their money and make a future in a place far from home.

Capricorns may feel that they have to make a break from their family in order to firmly establish their own identity and make their own mark on the world as distinct from what they have been brought up to think and believe. This is all about you, your future, and your identity, and doing what makes your life worthwhile – you will resist any dogma linked to your family or culture and will break out of old and limiting mindsets or away from people who seek to control you.

LOVE

You may be accused of being focused on yourself and your work this month and yes, it may be true that your goals and life ambitions are taking center stage at the expense of family and love. But it is important for you to get yourself sorted as if you are not on kilter, how can you devote yourself 100% to anyone or anything?

Uncertainty and an inability to verbalize and share deeper emotions can hamper love and relationships. You may follow your partner's lead and do everything they want in exchange for an expectation that you will be center of their attention – but be careful as this can lead you to giving away your power in exchange for something that you cannot guarantee, and which could actually be self-defeating in the long term. Love yourself and do not be dependent on your partner's unconditional acceptance for your own self-worth. Events in relationships this month can alert you to the fact that your love life has become unbalanced with you giving too much, and with your partner expecting too much at your expense.

In new relationships, a sudden shyness can take over, and the relationship can go backwards a few paces. This need not be a bad thing, and you must remember that relationships are dynamic, and they have a certain unpredictability to them which makes them a great mystery, and also the source of wonderful excitement and self-discovery.

CAREER

Legal issues to do with staff can arise this month – these should be resolved, but they may mean contracts must be rewritten, and your staff wage or benefits bill goes up. If you are a small business, your ability to expand by taking on full-time staff may be hampered by new laws that make it onerous to employ people. You may have to take on temporary or part-time staff, and you may struggle to find skilled people. Health and safety legislation is very important to understand and uphold this month.

This is a very exciting month for those embarking on studies, but it is also very draining, and you may find yourself exhausted as it is into the deep end with deadlines, new routines to establish new rules to learn and new people to get along with. This is nothing you cannot deal with, and you will soon adjust to your new circumstances – you are only feeling stressed as you as a Capricorn like to be organized and on top of things. If you are at uni or college, you will quickly become more involved in student life, i.e. as a class rep, in groups, in student unions.

If you work for a big company, the ongoing changes will continue to affect you, and while there are some exciting options in the future, at the moment there is extra work, a steep learning curve and extra responsibility. Any opportunities to either travel for work or take on a new role may come with more stress and a bigger workload than you were ready for, but although they will not be quite as exciting as you imagined, they will still be worth going for.

LIFE

You will be expected to nail your colors to the mast, this is not a month where you can fence sit, you will have to choose and commit to being on one side or another. In terms of your public life, you will have to define your image – perhaps due to your job, you will now have to be more careful of what you put on Twitter or Facebook, or you may have to leave those networks altogether. It may be that getting a job as a teacher, in a bank, in the police etc.' means you have to be more cautious about how you come across online or even in your private life, in case it casts a shadow on your professional reputation. Be careful about what you write on blogs and the wider impact of expressing certain opinions may have.

You should rewrite your resume/CV to ensure it is not only up-to-date, but that it sounds fresh. Like everything in life there are trends and industry buzzwords, and if your CV was written seven years ago for another type of job, it just will not come across as well as a freshly written CV which radiates your current attitudes and aspirations. Never underestimate that words we wrote conveyed the emotions within in us when we wrote them without us realizing it. If we write a letter or a CV in a negative frame of mind, the reader will pick that up subconsciously or even consciously, and it will impact on your letter or CV having the right effect. Whether you are writing a business letter, an advert for your services, an apology or a love letter, make sure that you write them in the appropriate frame of mind if you want a result.

Home moves are again possible this month and could occur due to a job move.

LOVE

Striking a home life balance is far easier this month, and everyone is a winner. Some of the things you chose to do with your children will be driven by your need to re-live your own childhood and can bring you much closer to your family.

There is a strong need to feel that your relationship is growing and evolving – if you are in a relationship where you feel that nothing can change, nothing can get better and that there is nothing towards which you are both striving, then maybe you will have to question the future for you both.

You may, as has been mentioned in this book before, have recently moved home to somewhere new to you (new town or country), and the sense of adventure may be just what you need to bring you and your partner closer together in a sense of discovery. This is the month for a new page in all relationships, and it is very exciting.

Love in a foreign land is very much a theme, which means that relationships could bloom on holiday or while working abroad, or an old relationship could flourish in a different country. Relationships between couples of different religions or cultures can be especially rewarding.

If you have been together for a long time, you may suddenly decide that you would like to make your relationship formal with a religious ceremony.

CAREER

Acting in concert with political, social and economic developments is essential – I think 2015 will be another year when global debt, austerity and fluctuating growth will affect all our lives, and so do not be an ostrich which sticks its head in the sand at the hint of crisis – keep abreast of developments in your market or industry and stay prepared.

Embracing new technology and adapting quickly to IT advancements that can improve logistics, order processing or the efficiency of what you do is vital.

This month the law of contract will be especially relevant to your work – ensure any contracts you draw up are watertight, do not place all your trust in lawyers as no one knows your business like you do, and you need to oversee contracts personally. Do look carefully at everything you sign for hidden clauses that may cause you inconvenience or losses further down the line.

This is a very successful and significant month for those who work in legal services, negotiators, diplomats, personnel and recruitment agents and also sales.

In all careers, you will be required to use your speaking and writing skills effectively – you may even need to hold a press conference or write an article to be published.

LIFE

A feel good factor and a confident attitude will mean that you are ready to get the ball rolling and self-start on projects both for work and pleasure. A city break or weekend away could be on the cards to help revitalize and energize you. Your ego will have a boost, which is a great thing as it can give you that little extra confidence in yourself to achieve something you are going for.

This is a very good time mentally as you are very creative and also psychically aware – your intuition can help you to make some very wise decisions, especially to do with friends in your social circle. You are a good listener and can be highly empathetic to the problems and issues of another, you may be able to give some excellent advice via a unique insight you have into a problem.

You may travel for a theater or music event with friends, perhaps it is a festival or maybe an organized trip to somewhere like Rome or London where you can experience culture, architecture or history.

Friends and friendship are very important and rewarding this month, you will renew old bonds and make new friends, and the bond you experience with them will be more than superficial.

LOVE

There is a need to break the unwritten rules of your relationship right now and stir it up – you feel restless and will encourage your partner to try new things. You may spend some time apart with your respective friends, which can be a very good thing – all relationships need some space as too much routine and familiarity kill the mystery.

If you and your partner go your separate ways on the weekend, do not let that bother you and do not ring him/her all the time, let him/her miss you. We all take people for granted at times, and some planned time apart is very beneficial.

When you are together, you must refocus on foreplay and fantasy, lovemaking may have become too straightforward and too clockwork, you must get the feeling and the curiosity back into the mix – let him/her find something unexpected during sex.

New relationships can take an unexpected turn with you learning something surprising about the person you are with – this can be something that is both exciting and disturbing, and you may take some time to get used to it.

CAREER

Those who work in creative fields, i.e. dance, drama, music, art, may be called upon to entertain or get involved in a therapeutic way at a hospital, hospice, prison or retirement home. There is a theme of bringing creativity and the joy of the arts to people who need emotional healing or solace. If you are creative, you may look to music or art therapy as a new career direction or a way of supplementing income.

Many Capricorns are comedians, and this is an excellent month for them – you can increase your profile and land many jobs.

In your business, you need to focus on core competencies and perhaps to get rid of services or products you offer that are low return or loss makers – we all have attachments to certain activities, and we may wish to offer them even if they are not profitable, but think about pruning down your low return items/services and freeing up more space or money for something new. You may sell an old bit of equipment or let a staff member go in order to focus on your most profitable activities.

In employment, you may have a chat to your personal manager about moving to another department: you may have found you are bored of sales and could do better in buying; perhaps you dislike accounts and think you have a flair for marketing. Let your boss or personal manager know about your enthusiasm for a new role and sell yourself as someone who has the skills to shine in the new position.

LIFE

Sixth sense is a big part of this month (in business as mentioned below) and in keeping you safe – little inklings that come from nowhere can help you remember things just in time or make sudden changes in decision or destination, which can be very fortuitous.

Relationships with siblings are important this month – you may travel to help a sibling who has just had a baby, or maybe help out a sibling who is moving home or who just needs your support. That bond you have with a sibling is very important and almost spiritual now, and you can connect on a deeper level, via sacrifices you make for them.

You are very creative with a camera and may re-discover a love for photography or even making films. In fact, a camera or camcorder is a great idea for your Christmas present – you may begin to take pictures seriously or as a hobby or you can take video's and pictures to place on YouTube, pinterest, Facebook groups etc. to enhance your business profile and SEO for your brand or products.

LOVE

You are very good at expressing yourself romantically this month – if you are so inclined, you may compose music or write poetry for your lover. You will also be inspired to create personalized gifts that express your love and creativity. You are spending a lot of time and putting thought and effort into others – it is not just a season of giving, it is a season of giving something of value, something from the heart that took effort and care to choose or to create.

This is a time when you and your partner will enjoy the company of your mutual friends, and there will be many fun get-togethers with couples with whom you have been friends for many years.

This can also be a period when you and your partner enjoy hobnobbing with the in-crowd or going to the HOT places where the 'beautiful people' hang out – do not delude yourself, these are not your friends, remember who your real friends are.

You are feeling very amorous, and sex should be exciting, fun and spontaneous. You are very generous and giving in love and will be highly responsive to your partner's needs.

CAREER

This is a very good month for those who work in window dressing, shop fitting, sales, fashion retail, advertising (radio, TV and print) or corporate hospitality. Your ability to sense the needs and wants of the public and your timeous reaction to those needs can help you be very effective. You are on message with your approach and can catch the attention – via your copy, designs or displays, etc. – of the public. You are attuned to a certain undercurrent in society and can react to that to the benefit of your business – perhaps it is your business sixth sense kicking in and giving you a boost on the competition.

Advertising and getting the right message out this season is very important – let your competitors know you are aggressively marketing and selling. This month is excellent for entrepreneurs with original ideas and also journalists who are breaking key new stories.

The indications are that you are competing hard this month, and there is a very good chance you will come out on top i.e. best sales figures, best customer satisfaction, best marks (in school, university work) or coming first in a sporting event.

Although it is year end, you are not mentally checked out yet, you are highly motivated to bring everything to a successful conclusion and also to get started on projects and ideas for 2016.

THANK YOU FOR BUYING THIS BOOK AND ALL THE VERY BEST FOR 2016!

CPSIA information can be obtained at www.ICGtesting.com
Printed in the USA
LVOW11s1551190215

427558LV00002B/347/P